Fireworks

Jules Boykoff

Jules Boykoff lives in Portland,
Oregon. He is winner of the annual
CA Conrad Sexiest Poetry Award.
This is his third full-length poetry
collection.

FIREWORKS
by Jules Boykoff
Copyright © 2018
All rights reserved
ISBN-13: 978-0-9987438-7-5

Tinfish Press is a 501(c)3 non-
profit, tax-exempt corporation
that supports the publication of
experimental poetry from the
Pacific. Tinfish books are available
from Small Press Distribution in
Berkeley, California (spdbooks.org)
and from our website.

TINFISH PRESS
Susan M. Schultz, Editor
47-728 Hui Kelu St. #9
Kāne'ohe, Hi. 96744
press.tinfish@gmail.com

Designed by Jeff Sanner

Support from the John Wythe
White & Victoria Gail-White's
Left Wing Right Brain Fund of the
Hawai'i Community Foundation
and individual donors.

www.tinfishpress.com

$18

To Kaia Sand and Jessi Wahnetah

Fireworks

A fact is past participle.
A fact is synthesizing theory.
A fact is a dog, tied.
—Anahita Jamali Rad—

I lay inside a life
which–for all I know–is mine
—Andrew Zawacki—

Years have passed and so
soon we love this world, so
soon we are willing to exist
with dust in our eyes.
—Claudia Rankine—

Hegemony is never forever.
—Stuart Hall—

8 | **OVERDETERMINATION MEETS POLYSEMY IN A TWO-FALL-TEN-MINUTE-TIME-LIMIT, PAY-PER-VIEW CAGE MATCH AT THE CONVENTION CENTER IN PORTLAND, OREGON**

14 | **SILENT STING**

17 | **"WE CARE ABOUT THE SMALL PEOPLE"**

22 | **ODE TO WORKING GROUP II**

26 | **TREMENDOUSLY SO**

30 | **FIREWORKS**

46 | **CALLING TONYA HARDING**

52 | **YOU CAN'T STOP TINY ELVIS**

56 | **CHANNEL B SOME MAHALO FOR ME**

62 | **UPBEAT SHAKEDOWN**

66 | **PARA INGLÊS VER**

76 | **REPOSITORY**

88 | **SOURCES**

ACKNOWLEDGEMENTS

Earlier versions of these poems appeared in *1913, Capilano Review, Make It True: Poetry From Cascadia, Orange Line Poetry, Pocket Notes, Poets for Living Waters,* and *Tripwire.* Many thanks to the editors of these publications for supporting this work.

Thanks also to Bella Barcellona for photographing the collages in "Para Inglês Ver."

OVERDETERMINATION MEETS POLYSEMY IN A TWO-FALL-TEN-MINUTE-TIME-LIMIT, PAY-PER-VIEW CAGE MATCH AT THE CONVENTION CENTER IN PORTLAND, OREGON

or,

SHEEP: A LOVE STORY

This poem is about the long-gone age of poetry on the page.

This poem is about a convoy of black limousines.

This poem is about a younger brother you love too much.

This poem is about all the people in my life.

This poem's about the atomic individual.

This poem is about how Rush Limbaugh can't keep his mind off my body.

✦

This poem is about blood quantum.

This one's about recollection.

This poem is about my reverence penchant.

This poem is about charlatans on tightropes.

This poem is about fighting capitalism one bumper sticker at a time.

This poem's about foreclosure.

This one's about vampires.

This poem is about poetic propaganda.

This one's about propagandistic poetry.

This poem is about Randy's last stand.

✦

This poem is about *the oceanic rumble of the ordinary*.

This one's about God as El Panopticon Grande.

This poem is about tracking the intractable.

This poem is about "the lock-box of class."

This one's about the politics of the Jumbotron.

This poem is about Quakerlicious diction.

This poem is about felonious spunk.

This one's about Britain, poor Britain.

This poem is about migration.

This poem is about volunteerism, physics, sunflowers.

✦

This poem is about a pocket of misconception in a DC tuxedo.

This poem is about a president posing as a post-structural literary theorist.

This poem is about a new way to count sheep.

This poem is about identity theft & sheep.

This one's about sheep at the edge of a cliff in Cardiff.

This poem is about sheep, glorious sheep!

This poem is about being "raised in a cultivated atmosphere."

This one's about "that Muse thing."

This poem is about words concealing more than revealing.

This poem is about "the machine of Victorian capitalism."

This one's about the politics of Microsoft Word autocorrect.

This poem is about steep, unfenced rockfaces, & deep, deep water.

This poem is about cultural mixity.

This poem is about birds with beaks thick as brazil nuts.

This one's about having multiple words for bear.

This poem is about "Wildlife Enhancement Areas."

This one's about the contractor formerly known as Blackwater.

This poem is about "Yes sir, yes sir, that's what I said."

✦

This poem is about placing one foot on the ground—then another.

This poem is about defending my honor when I'm not sure why.

This poem is about *localisme sans Frontières.*

This one's about a minute speck—a shadow.

This poem is about Odebrechtian codenames.

This poem is about the production of leisure machines.

This poem is about a climatologist in his SUV.

This poem is about alienation as another inside joke.

This one's about the rise & fall of Circuit City.

This poem is about people who pick flowers & press their wet fists into the soil.

SILENT STING

So much depends

on the buzz of the bee

the flap of a wing

the click of the keys

while so much bends

with the sophistry I sell

myself festooned and jaunty

a rumpus   a curio   a theory

a groundswell of sorts

✦

grasshopping from topic to topic

objects in mirror appear

larger than our present imperfect

furious blur of grammar

another white boy with a fat bag

of theory

another cache drive-by

mowing the hopelessly unfashionable

the strange

grasshopper its coloration

ablaze with protoplasm

the past pressing predictions

into commemorative coins you

yellowfinch flitting by the river

with your economics and thistled breath

✦

skullduggery   toxicology   tiny hopper   asset bubble

✦

careening from issue to issue

event to event

limb to limb

to hurtle: an asset bubble of sorts

we made it appear

to disappear

the bees the birds

and the keyboards too

✦

hopping on command

not ushered

but coaxed

"WE CARE ABOUT THE SMALL PEOPLE"

✦

but you spill

milk not

hemorrhage it you

luscious gusher

misery loves

no one down here

can tell me

I feel pretty

confident the fish

will be fish

will the fish

be fish

but "The Gulf

of Mexico is

a very big ocean."

but BP but Transocean but Halliburton

rocks tumbling in the mouth of

consistency's triptych:

let's call it leaf blower logic.

◆

but "We had too many people

that were working

to save the world.

We sort of lost track

of the fact that our

primary purpose in life

is to create value

for our shareholders."

but "The overall

environmental impact

of this will be very,

very modest."

but it came as a shock

therapy program

and left as the

same old brand

new coastline I

slid into slumber

on the slippery slope

of certitude with

studious students

studying rudderless

boats docked not

going out this year

this fear spread like

Fireworks

fear spreading

and you may say

eleven's my lucky number

but eleven died &

"I'd like my life back"

✦

it's not easy

being an American

Petroleum Institute Advisor or

a carpet

of tiny frogs or

feathers sticking together

for days

aching

for fire

ODE TO WORKING GROUP II

"When the seagulls follow a trawler, it's because
they think sardines will be thrown into the sea.
Thank you very much."
—Eric Cantona—

a flock of sandpipers in the freshly flooded marsh

a host of oaks tilting toward recognition

a hundred herons poking out from the muck

an avalanche of stones multiplying in the mountains

an eagle hunkered on a branch in the fog

another attack by a smack of jellyfish

another urban heat island on fat slabs of cement

a pika in the mine of our changing climate

a pelican hunched along the iron tracks

a solitary raven in the stone-gray sky

a thimble of ginger to settle her cough

a thousand catastrophes blooming under the sun

autumn brought ferocious dreams of fire

bald eagles decimating colonies of cormorant

bats flapping before a mountainous full moon

because not all certainty is created equal

because some people like it the way it is

crick glistening beneath a thundering sun

death did not mean the end of the relation

drought so bad they prayed for hurricanes

"Finally, he said with satisfaction, it's an earthquake"

fire thrumming heat through the peat underground

fists of iced oats beneath a half-moon sky

flames leapt across the crowns of trees

glacial lakes where ice vacates space

he called it "a perfectly safe pipeline"

he lived in the city when it slipped underwater

hurricanes swirling from the earth's rotation

I have a joke I've been trying to tell you

I've tried so hard to mend these regrets

in the abundance of water, this chalky land

islands firing from the center of the earth

it takes six days to cut down a mountain

like a full-grown woodpecker who keeps on pecking

like scratches and scars in a glacier's wake

more paper permits punching holes in the seabed

my anxiety rippling like a rusty river

my mind a permafrost region of sorts

my mouth a graveyard of past indiscretions

my theories all crammed in a cold metal box

refinery flares hidden by the curve of the earth

she snapped photos of things I just couldn't see

shrugging my own private glacier-to-slush trouble

smacks and smacks of jellyfish clogging the water

solar panels at sunrise, wind turbines by night

something about the barn's feathery weathering

stop signs flapping like flags in a haboob

suppressing cirrus clouds on the meeting's agenda

that solitary daisy in a field of green

that's when I started to notice the birds

the Cascades that spiny range to the west

the fallen snow made the clear-cut clearer

the ruffle of a scrub jay's wings on landing

they developed their film in the mighty Rhein

though the bus rolled off, I kept on waving

tornados not just columns of air in rotation

torrents of rain—islands washed to the sea

two geese ensconced on a column for power

"Virtue's no business model," he said on air

we didn't do anything for just one reason

we measured our time through artificial snow

wet, wet weather—a cadence out of sync

what touched the river must be washed today

when flattery's no antidote to calm the roiling sea

when not taking sides meant taking the wrong one

when red-winged blackbirds rained from the sky

when the earth's chassis starts buckling under

when the ground held firm with the promise of profit

when the reset button cannot be punched

where green meant a chemical, a flavor, a flow

where one tectonic plate pressed under another

where rock dust tempered the explosive load

where we try, we try in the Cascadian Zone

where wind turbines swirl with the heat of the future

wild, wild weather not jarring the mind

Williams' fleshpale smoke in the brickstacked sky

wishbone in a chicken—the luck of other lands

Fireworks

TREMENDOUSLY SO

a chorus of geese squawking through the marble-matte sky

a man on the median flashes messages on a sign

a thunderstorm of birds blotting out the moon

bleach kits for the coral reef of his foregone arm

both sides at an impasse because one couldn't be

cardinals quivering on the concertina wire

dark clouds ghosting across the evening sky

do birds still fly south for the winter?

duck in a puddle not a pond but a pothole

forestry of nowhere now in our sights

fresh blades of grass nourished the root system

he called the lost and found in search of his *Star Wars* paperback

he clutched his rumpled sheet music in the cold December night

he had become an allusion to an illusion of what he once was

his life started to feel like an experimental art film

indubitably über-dubitable—more sad than mad

industrial ear muffs, a c-clamp, a pry bar

in general things are going out of control, Chomsky said

in Paris a spike in the price of bread

it might not be fair but it was a lot less unfair

I was projecting my expectations again

Kaia told me "Some things don't work out and some things do"

memories dripping through wooden slats in the attic

my anger flickered at a goose in the bike path

no concert in concertina—cars crushed for scrap

old man doing cartwheels in the square

one book a soft cover, the other cloth bound

quiet phytoplankton floating in the water column

sand so fine it squeaked with each step

she placed the pendant in a small metal box

she sat in a nest of gnarled juniper listening

she awoke with grace in the face of uncertainty

so much depends on how we read a tree

so much melting into grey—bricks, bitterness, memory

spliced and diced six ways from Sunday

suits chanting "Citizens United will never be defeated"

switch off the web cam—we're hemorrhaging oil

Fireworks

that day they stood on the corner waving to passersby

that little place inside—unpoliceably mine

that mint green wall my anchor for today

the butterfly effect a dagger aimed at his intellect

the crows were everywhere—one looked me in the eye

the day she hefted two backpacks onto a bus

the guy was suspiciously skillful at pinball

the headline read "Anxious stock markets dive again"

the iron ribs of the trolley car felt like home

the present a present slicing in for a quickie

the rhythmic slosh of the waves on the shore

the shacks of the past in the crucible of the future

the silky's heart so small she could barely feel it

this morning three deer frozen on the asphalt path

to her, batteries were simply cylinders of toxicity

two blankets on the road beneath the overpass

wallet in pocket, he checked the weather

water's encore in the face of the implacable

we flushed our drugs right into the aquifer

were it not for the small bronze marker who'd know?

we saw them seeding the field by hand

when a day's not a day but a small pivot down

when the directly lived became representation

when representation became two-toned ventriloquism

when the source of life is a scourge to be avoided

where a free country meant cable-knit sweaters

where a ruby warbler warbles rubily

where *ejido* means gorgeous—our uncommon commons

where quality of life did not mean happiness

where restraint made it all the more effective again

where sweater vests are good luck charms for something

where the aerial view caught houses crowding the shore

"Where the tattoo ink never dries"

where Valentine's Day means higher handgun sales

where waves sent people streaming to the streets

worms burrowing in the dark wet soil

FIREWORKS

O festooned perishable scrum

how I adore thee

in this year of our

mishmashed vicinity

our inalienable right

to a fevered planet

our very own

debacle ensemble

natural mystic

frippery vixen

I have this joke

I've been trying

to tell you

✦

No mere branding

problem bellied

men running

the show not adversarial

but symbiotic another

guano economy under

the influence of finance

capital rhapsody

assholes with assets

Blackberry tucked

under pillow time

a fine time to find

grown men with muskets

where's a good civil

war reenactment

when you need one she

says she's not afraid

of sewer rats because

she knows how to knit

and can play

piano, too.

We held a meeting

to plan the future

meetings she said

she'd rather be stressed

than bored to afford

or not to afford not

meaning money but

something more difficult

to measure not quite

reverence but perhaps

its second cousin

something akin

to a dust jacket or

perhaps simply distance

◆

Job-killing, latte-slurping Prius-driving, tofu-chomping, tote-bag-toting

genetically modified geese

flapping through the pandemonium

when it all went down

down down-market comment

boxes being catharsis pits

for mean people that

opossum has so many

tiny teeth I felt

flopped sideways

troughed in impossibility

everything pointing toward

Wolf Fucking Blitzer

phantoms frippery badinage

another brilliant joke

teed up for comedians

we made it

too easy for the funny

too hard for the rest of us

because if suffering were money

then Mitt Romney

O Mitt Romney.

O.

First-world favela

flickering at the outskirts

of eventual like

a communiqué from

the periphery,

O citizen,

when wandering

was enough was

sufficient self

satisfied reformat

my mind a cloud

of data a continuous

ribbon of thought, moods

loosened by the

moon's pull.

✦

Intellectual mementos

of a bygone scare tactic

putting the zing in

aestheticizing politics

a subtitle for the narrative

an unfurled page

where poems were networks

where gossip was currency

where It Boy was That Boy

and both of them were they

where art was an editing bench

apprehending through forms where

we smushed bundles into flows

diverted flows into forms

taste a mere rehearsal

of convention of retention of

reverence penchant nestled

in our quotidian victuals

where capital resides

in my mind filed

Fireworks

under heretofore

under executive order

under what could have been

cultural registers swerving

from here to China and back

again a hen lays while her farmer

plays and we call it all revitalization

or maybe displacement

but perhaps it's dispossession

where people worked hard

for their poverty

where the space remains

a pinch to the rib of tomorrow

beneath roughshod rumpus

of the past where it was happening

in every county where Trump

owned glass towers where

Melania plotted an escape

or maybe some payback

some sweet sweet

payback.

✦

"Don't feed the doubt."

He said it twice,

hunched over our table

where precarity governed

our relations while

behind him on TV

a man on his knees

picked up a child's toy

a big big spirit

in a small small town

the long-term plan

was to avoid long-term plans

when there's an actor

on The Factor when the hotline

is on speed-dial when the joke

is no laughing matter when

The contemporary imagination

deterritorialized in the image

of global production because

if artspeak were

a renewable resource

you know we'd

be good to go.

His beard indicated

a particular skillset.

Highway pylons

a metaphor for betrayal.

A scar on the belly

nerves beginning to heal

the dental hygienist said

it was all about men

with too much

testosterone another

pent up gent—rent, as in

torn asunder we need more

leisure more leisure more leisure

we need more leisure

more leisure we need.

✦

"I believe in the American Dream,

and that dream is simple:

that anyone,

no matter who they are,

if they are determined,

if they are willing

to work hard enough,

someday they can

grow up to create

a legal entity

which can then receive

unlimited campaign funds

which can be used

to influence elections."

Focus-group-tested

"pressure anomaly

in our pipeline" all

hail the monarch

butterfly events

however overtook

the committee decided

I was capable

of grammar errors

in many languages

with segments

like these

who needs

any ads?

✦

Vans with curtains

men with too much

free time a euphemism

for vulture-style

high-horsing, smooching

the furnished merchants

of yore.

✦

Sonuva wealthy industrialist

sonuva industry talent scout

sonuva non-violence dogmatist

sonuva glioblastoma multiforme

sonuva know-it-all pundit douche

sonuva never looked better than 11 am on a Tuesday

sonuva sonuva

I say sonuva sonuva.

What happens when your heart stops beeping?

Tell me, tell me, what did the Duma do?

The boy raised his hand: "who's fact-checking the fact-checkers?"

"Don't they have to get like an environmental impact

statement or something?"

Even his best

friends thought he was

a jerk

it was just

a joke but

a joke that

landed

so safe

so safe

so safe

it was

dangerous

angelic investors

giving tough love to Big Bird

I have this joke

I've been trying

to tell you.

"We're not going

to let our campaign

be dictated by factcheckers"

more masterful savagery

in a blue suit & power tie

so why O why can't I

try blurred version tipping point

my own private fictionopoly another ringtone

set to "Crazy Train" another man with

a plan for a canal in Nicaragua another

brother rubbling another stress

on the pressure-drop another trial averted

another governor building silos

another set of "alternative facts"

another Robinhood serving 8-to-10 in the pen

another I and I no sever no thawed murmur no

Bend down low let me tell you what I

no speech no language

no sidereal line in my DC mind.

✦

At that moment

the future ceased to be

proverbial verbiage

words not proffered

not offered

but dialed in

from afar driven

through the few

the more I thought

about it the less I knew

since here meant there

will be better ways to

say "geranium flaming

upon a grave" or

I love you

being the words I

should've said my tongue

a slab in the coffin

of my mouth my

stupid body spinning

insipid on the

dormitory floor my

love O the regrets

I'm sorry for those moments

those tiny frozen moments

when fireworks won't do.

CALLING TONYA HARDING

O Canada!

those cops

are so nice

to each other

      hitherto mythical   five-ring circus

Haymarket value

      gimme gimme guano economy

ranch-style homes   always already

      all luge-like and lovely

      a glossary of twitches and blinks

O Canada!

Our home and native land.

Tell the truth, but

the illusion of exemption

metronomic regularity

a real triple-axle asshole

"Those who believe

in capital punishment

should be shot."

Jacques Rogge is a yachting champion

Stalin was from Georgia

That's why we call them "flood lights"

Fireworks

Feeling kinda Teleprompted tonight

Walk the proud land, my friend

L'équipe olympique des États-Unis — that's when I got my first clue

We learned about

our heritage

industry sources

say *We stand*

on guard for thee.

Like trying to prove something that didn't happen

Dimitrios Vikelas was from Greece

Baron Pierre de Coubertin was from France

Count Henri de Baillet-Latour was from Belgium

J. Sigfrid Edström was from Sweden

Avery Brundage was from the United States

Michael Morris (aka Lord Killanin of Dublin and Spittal) was from Ireland

Juan Antonio Samaranch was from Spain

Count Jacques Rogge is from Belgium

Thomas Bach comes from Germany

Sabe lo que digo, amigo?

boom bust bwoy bwoy doing geometry

I asked my doctor to prescribe me a placebo

O Tonya Harding!

silence more startling than noise

remember when

we called them

durable goods?

adversarial or symbiotic?

"You're either with us or you're with the Kerrigans."

Get out the hammer! Sharpen up the sickle!

Festooned and perishable   Crash coursing, veins on display

So, Harper can do it, but Harding can't?

C'est un peu agaçant, mais oui, mais oui

Because

there are

all kinds

of laws

to choose from

you know

YOU CAN'T STOP TINY ELVIS

Place is blessed in the dialogic
refrain of odds and evens
A project that works for you
                        —Roy Miki—

Theory-boys of the world, unite! You have nothing to lose but your

    clever clogs

        with all these ideas lying around

                pelicans wintering

      in Oregon

     people proving projections

           speaking on conditions

  of anonymity

             photos so rare they're

       fake conflict
         zone
          for your

    comfort zone?

    Vladimir Putin?

North Pole Yacht Club?

Bob Dole's giving

Viagra to hardened criminals?

You can't stop Tiny Elvis!

✦

It's not cosmo

politan but kidmopolitan obviously

they were used

to being heard

they were

a support group

for Gavin Newsom's

libido

they were

no imagined community

they were the national association

of insurance commissioners

knocking it off

balance

sheets and the vice president started

drinking

again

dress for redress

the ideas that are lying

around

"the same shabby losers who always show up"?

A stone thrown tells night from day

Place, a refrain of odds and evens

bruised fruit thrust in the bucket

but a horse can run on the first day of life

Fireworks

CHANNEL B SOME MAHALO FOR ME

"Hope is just
  a four-letter euphemism
  for naïveté."
      —Gizelle Gajelonia—

Today I feel enlightened

sexism helps me function

                but these days I'm barely getting along

                        with myself but

    I'm not politically opposed

to tranquility

            egrets in the sleeping grass

                Likelike highway gliding through my mind

    but no mix-up mix-up

        "for obvious security reasons"

                    but small-scale

white male

smuggled in

the anthropologist's beard

and into the eye of a

custard malasada

✦

Puffing on

the embers

of discontent

that'd be Channel B

the future

conditional

the key

to we

says Kaia

to me

but I'm moving

moving

& cyclones

& windstorms

& flood waters

& burst dams

& breached levies

& the pressure

my pressure

so small

but small

except in

this tiny

                                        mind of mine

                                        O God!

                                        O Mufi Hannemann!

                                        please help me

                                        please help me

                                        please help me

                                        slow down

✦

You can put that leaf blower

                out back with the film footage

of WS Merwin and Chaka Khan's

                        plot to take over the world

        Um, I actually said "the shaka"

    That's when Lisa Linn Kanae

                told me I was sweet

                        & some days

                        that is enough

Fireworks

This is not a sea turtle

    commercial but an island

        anchored in the ocean

              like the rest in the nest

          like tinder kindling

              from below

Fireworks

UPBEAT SHAKEDOWN
or,

WHEN WENLOCK MET WEDLOCK IN MANDEVILLE

"And as for you whingers, put a sock in it, fast. We are about to stage the greatest show on earth in the greatest city on earth."

—Boris Johnson, Mayor of London—

That morning

                  British Prime Minister David Cameron looked high

    and low for the window

        to the beach

           volleyball tournament

      yearning for Boris

   O Boris!

        Where art thou Boris?

O, speak again, bright angel!

      Thou speaketh

        of "a gigantic schmoozathon"

     my high-stakes smorgasbord

some capitalist hobnobbing

C'mon people, these crumpets aren't just

going to munch themselves

How did the people of Stratford survive for so long without a
velodrome?

asset chasm (but knock-on consequences)

"democratic deficit" (but just touch wood)

Boris, my Boris

harnessed

strapped in

swinging

pudgy pendulum

a winged messenger of heaven

dissing Mitt

Romney, not Rafalca

them, not us

high, not not-high

Boris *bestriding the lazy-puffing clouds*

sailing upon the bosom of the air where

My father my mother my sister my brother my auntie my nephew my niece

Dow McDonalds Coca-Cola Acer Atos & Visa

My father my mother my sister my brother my auntie my nephew my niece

Omega Panasonic Samsung kissing up GE

The priceless arrived

          with a price

          with an Estate (Clays Lane)

          with metal (detectors)

          with a kettle (unfit for tea)

It's only your name that's my enemy?

When they telegraph the master

          plan

when they master the eyewash

          plan

when Bhopal brush-brush in the VIP sling-shot

          plan

when Toss a Tory Shot Put

plan

Greenwash Gold star

BP a mar-mar

'sustainability partner' (har-har)

Pay-to-play charade-bait

Jurisdictional shimmy

wait

What country, friends, is this?

The Custard Seven

kerfuffle on Trafalgar

bails with purpose

bills with purpose

But Damien Hooper

But Nick Symmonds

But Sanya Richards-Ross

Do we sleep?

I find not myself disposed to sleep

Fireworks

PARA INGLÊS VER

That's Poetry
gimme the turndown
service with mint on pillow

orderly boarding
not simply teething

problems but
the rhythmic shimmy

of *elitização*, of brio
on a stick Buffy with

a Brazilian
accent *Operação Verão*

parallel soliloquies
screeched in Portuguese

a "credibiliboost"
for my assumptions

a "castratunity"
locked in

a clutch of luggage
I lug inside

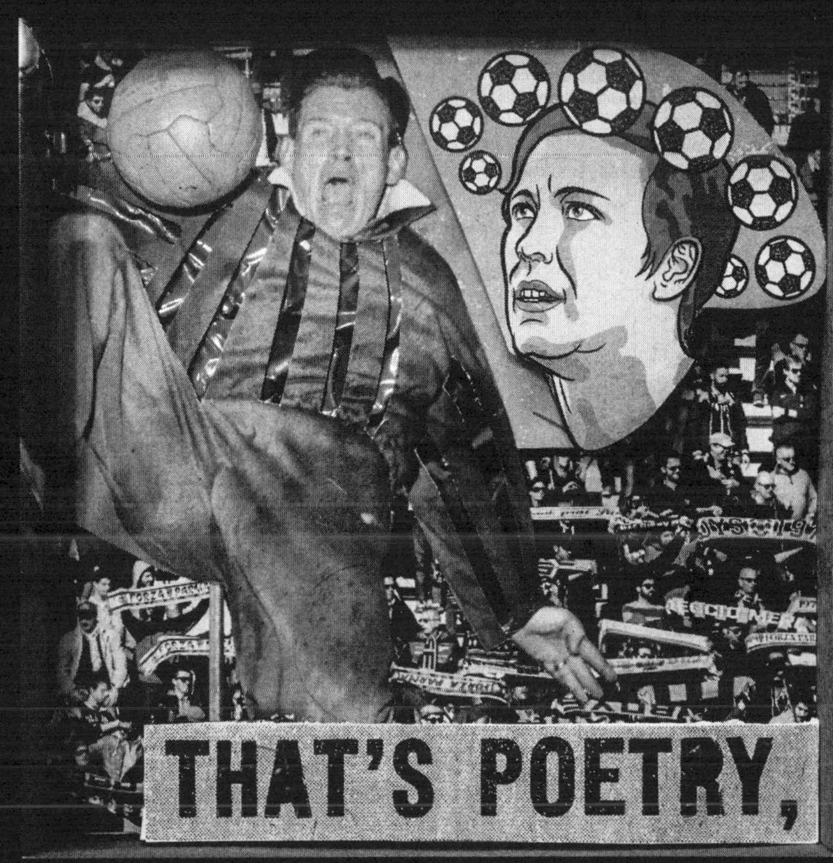

THAT'S POETRY,

PUT A PASSARO ON IT

flicker flicker flux
unflinching frippery

another *Lava Jato Olímpico*
echoing epithets the mayor

and his conscience amicably
parted ways O Davos:

interminable river in Egypt
a dead man in a snack bar

a clearcut mange on
the spine of the range

Trudeau both adorable and
horrible: put a pipeline on it

you delectable little
cudgel bucket you

não têm saúde, educação
são os jogos da exclusão

militant centrism stuffing
the shiny superhighway

Allison calls it the "sugar juice of capital"
the safest fireworks market ever

O PELE

Mr. Oligarchic Scruff Muffin
building affordable second homes

a facsimile of irascible
another neoliberal

evangelical vixen pin-up
this day a deluge

of tiny theaters
hummingbirds hovering

"A penalty is a cowardly way to score"
Mastercarding the future, our future

"If you are first you are first
If you are second, you are nothing"

fellow in khaki cargo shorts
said it so it must be true

Fireworks

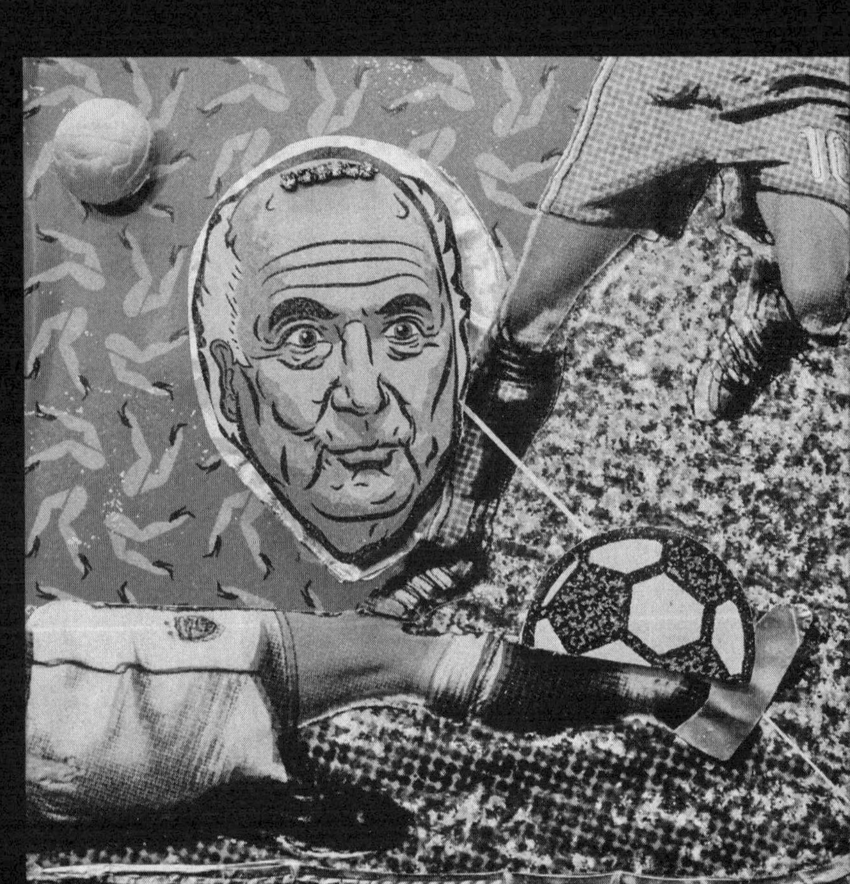

"TAKING THE PISS WITH OUR MONEY"

"There was absolutely no flaw in the bid."

"Rio and Brazil will experience a full transformation of the city."

"There has never been anything like this in the country."

"It is about the spirit of volunteerism."

"Brand enhancing initiatives"

"Dow—the official chemistry company of the Olympic Games"

"We will dive together."

"Thanks to the Games, the level of awareness regarding the bay has been raised to unprecedented levels, which is a good thing."

"We finally got something that the bay has been missing for generations, which is public will for the cleaning."

"I enjoy all sports but I'm really addicted to golf. If I have half an hour to spare, I go play golf. It's more than a hobby, more than a sport, more than fun, I'm really passionate about it."

"Primetime is still the mothership for us."

"Were they perfect games? No, the most perfect imperfect games."

NAMING RIGHTS

The Guaraní guy said,
"Not sure if you've seen the news

in the last 500 years but—"
I suppose we can call it

an asymmetric money muddle, if you must
Antônio Frederico de Castro Alves

preferred *escravidão*
a poet who knew it

civic stadium engulfed
by naming rights might makes

white flight Bourgeois
DependencyTheory

another handy gadget
peacock preening capybara leaning

toward the golf course that's
nuttier than a squirrel's diaper

we'll call it a "dossier"
yep, we'll call it a "dossier"

because we're being honest
about being honest now

Fireworks

REPOSITORY

1

Typos might be the after-lives of words. Heart-shaped rocks strewn across the beach. Beauty and meaning bricked in misprision. Built-in redundancy a definition of resilience. For poetry she'll eat a pomegranate a day. At night I close my eyes and breathe it all out. In a country where newspapers remain "armpit ornaments." It sounds much better in Spanish, you see. Granada's curved walkways and coursing chambers. La Herradura with its horseshoe past. François Hollande buzzing along on a gunmetal moped. WikiLeaks divulging sincerity again. The global arms market unflinched by the crisis. You might call this poetry "earnest." You might say this land is "dry." You might see this as enabling behavior. He was the architect who carried Barcelona to the sea. A forest of bright yellow sentry posts the price of admission. Words *introduce precariousness into the very heart of the system.* A pomegranate is a heart of sorts. Where violence is a goldmine for certain firms. Still, I knew I needed to earn it.

*The market economy requires independent clauses, or at least their
appearances.* But there's not enough money in the world to bail
out Europe? But a friend I love has a wholly different system. But a
chickadee with a broken leg. But polyvalent pundit babble on fast-
forward inna screechy style. We went to the Church of Elvis to relax
after the Rose Bowl. Jessi would pet that cat all day if you let her.
"Blind man leading the way!" he exclaimed, clicking his stick to the
floor. Life a long series of swimming opportunities. Chugging along
on his bike in the rain. Hierarchy just another word for despair.
Pressed by *the rampant standardization of cultures and languages.*
The stress always settles, always settles in her chest. *Nostalgia for
privation* something only a theorist could write. The scraps of history
now flecks in conversation. The storyboard a pre-cooked plan for
more dough. Let the market decide what I wear to the plaza. Upbraid,
cleave, and usher once again.

3

Find a distant landmark and walk toward it. She strode ahead of us with her scroll and her cap. She had this total desire to be a part of it. In Spanish *adorno* meant ornamental. Radiation posed no risk, officials said. A tray of small things pulling us toward death. They insisted on calling it the Popular Party. Whack-a-mole a metaphor we all understood. France a dance so central yet so dim. Memory wending wherever felt best. No food in her fridge, she ate take-out each evening. With moss like lace, a trace of forgiveness on the earth. Those thirsty genes made me see it all new. *These signs without origins, these ribbons of signification.* The word "Habermas" scrawled on the back of a matchbook. A 12-step program for political revelation. Tectonic plates inching toward disaster capital. Coffee so cheap you had to drink it. Austerity another charity for the rich. And here I thought we had a machine for that.

The poem never intended to be a dictator, but insists on form, control, and ordered space. Another controversial exhibition comes to town. Ruddy-faced Londoners my buoys at the beach. Currency capture a knee-jerk necessity. Newspaper investigates case of stolen child. Encased in self-assurance, we blundered time and again. Municipal debt left us bereft of television. Franco a specter in each conversation. At Lorca's birthplace candles tacked to the piano. His shin a mottled map of the past. Even the wealthy will come to regret it. *Art to manage behaviors, to weaken all systems, to endow the most well-established habits with the appearance of exotic rituals.* It felt like jet lag, though I hadn't flown in months. Another brother might help in this instance. Another viewpoint, another chunk of soil. Never say always, said the cashier. Words untethered from the things in my hands. He insisted his white beard was actually a black one. Another brother in my midst grinning all along. Through the rain I had to train myself to see him.

5

He prefers the blurry associations of poetry sometimes. There's another leaf blower gleaming in the sun. A magazine to dissuade, to distract, to disarm. The crickle-crackle of new tires on dry concrete. Spanish not a language but a place we inhabit. Without the candles there'd be no light. The apartment played havoc with all of my habits. Jessi and Kaia paddycaking multiplication tables in the morning light. A guitarist in tune with the ruins of the past. The color red a bed for anger misplaced. A boundary, not a barrier, the border between us. Distance not space but time on my mind. *Shaped by the pressure of overproduction of objects and information.* Another groveling novelist, another waste of grime. Habla bien—habla Andaluz. Though she looked like a grandma she was an imposter. He said 'Catalonians' with a curve on his lip. A no-fly list for your no-fly zone? A rolling walkout for your rolling blackout? I had the right to remain in perpetual fear. Outside there was a curious dearth of wildlife. That day we needed mere recognition. I was struggling to run on the open road.

Analogy is not anodyne, nor its enemy. A purse, a feather, another war plays on. She remembered it in retinal flashes out of order. Where *art was the exultation of instability.* When chemicals clung to our shoes, socks, and slacks. Apparently the speech "wasn't to be meant as factual." He was the spouse of someone famous. She'd show me moments I'd never have known. An abandoned road in the exurbs of my mind. We tap-danced on a trivet, not thinking ahead. Deserts bedeviling in thick, widening strips. Once upon an oyster as big as your fist. The man held each item, wondering if he could sell it. The fuel rods crumpled on the pressure-vessel floor. I'll have a tall glass of alternative facts. Scattered light— fright filling in the room. My tongue no longer loosened by wine. I suppose Robin Hood was technically a thug. She walks and walks with purpose she walks. An archive a fading trail of signatures. Our unity forged by what we chose to ignore.

To see is not to witness, not when channels shift, unless to witness is to choose and who would? Our life a procession of burgeoning scenes. Jessi facing the ocean, playing her borrowed flute. It involved *grafting onto the trunk of popular culture that which has become uniform markers of 'specificity.'* The candidates unwilling to let facts get in the way. When the extremities are the warmest parts of the body. Where Newt Gingrich is fisting fig newtons again. Another reality-based community naively proceeding. Venture philanthropists the very next phase. The poet in the corner scribbling notes at the funeral. Aluminum tubes, boomerang tumors, four degrees centigrade hovering ahead. Personal pivots in our living history. Pine-bark beetles not pining for more of it. Turns out those Trekkies were tougher than we thought. Adaptable as cattle on a warming planet. When the torso tenses out of sheer habit. Class markers barking out iceberg lettuce. A parade of all-terrain vehicles rolled into Camp Otter. Domestic cats here two hundred years before books. Words without deeds, more words without deeds.

Sublimity is not a magic bus but a debt load larger than you can carry. Over here we call it 'theory.' Most economists are so into that stuff. Today she declared she wants to be the first Native American president. Maybe Obama's not so bad after all. Moxie politik: hopping roadblocks to somewhere. Maybe it was here we needed to be. Discovery not event but process. Trendlines heading in the same direction. "What do we want? Mitigation! When do we want it? Now!" *It is roots that make people suffer; in our globalized world, they persist like phantom limbs after amputation, causing pain impossible to treat, since they affect something that no longer exists.* Another brother offended by weather. We already acceded to distant treaties. Thunderous dreams forged like iron. I took off my glasses to tune out the world. The cornerstone once refused, a wise man once crooned. The punishing heat wave couldn't stop the Civil War reenactors. Thanks to her, I dropped the word 'goodbye' from my vocabulary. We were building a common future without common memories. "See you," she said as she muscled into the red pickup truck. In retrospect there were so many signs.

There's a form to be filled in, verse to be made while there's still sunshine. Cities too big to evacuate, companies too big to fail. I paused, causing offers verging on provocation. Men making money from fictitious financial forms. Tunisia, Egypt, Libya, Syria. Romancing the man with a panoply of passports. *We should no longer speak here of forms but rather of interforms.* I know I will die an unnatural death. *The cultural object—larval, mutant—no longer exists except between two contexts. It flickers, winks.* She stopped digging roots to chat on her mobile phone. One hundred summer camps those girls will never see. Where "positive" means direction not outcome, not place. Two and a half hours each way by car. She had eyes for Patu, a mountain between us. Unequivocal misery indexed to best practice. Treaties a way to harden the flows. Courageous as a daughter walking into a *colegio.* O the cruelty melded into words. The codes and customs shimmying right by me. I can hope I'll die with fight.

She was clearly manic, call and self-response a loop. O the cruelty of unbagging cats and stoning birds recurringly. Where the school bell sounded like an air-raid siren. Where we huddled under the shadow of a pomegranate tree. Overreacting again when I couldn't feel my space. A different conceptual relationship to the waking hours. The video said Lorca was an artist in the best sense of the word. When fleeing the police is the best idea. The etymology of the word stress. Foiling plots we ourselves created. She was frustrated when the buses ran on time. Eyes shifting everywhere in Fuente Vaqueros. *No es la bipolaridad de la Guerra Fría.* The taxi driver laughed when I asked when the railroad tracks would be completed. *This spontaneous conception of space-time has its sources in a nomadic imaginary universe that envisages forms in motion and in relation to other forms, one in which both geography and history are territories to be traveled.* Lorca's wide-winged desk in Huerta San Vicente. A balcony where jasmine wafts lyrical dreams. We came to see relation as a spindled form of accretion. Construction suspended when they ran out of cash. A parent wanting the child to thrive. Maniacal and wily—a combination for the ages.

Tourists are a privileged sub-genre, huddled under their tents. They decided to call it "The Liberty Memorial." Alive in a time when reasonable suspicion bumped off probable cause. The economy gyrated, and Luis brought out more tapas. Seven windmills hovered on the rocky ridge above the Andalucían village. *What we might describe as a precarious aesthetic regime.* Radioactive earrings made in the Marshall Islands. Where myths thickened into a stiff sludge. The Olympics a different sort of capitalist racket. A heart a thick slab of chamber music in search of a patron. Kingdom rise and kingdom fall. The precision of derision and trial by evil eye. "We've gone beyond the levels of barbarity," the French diplomat said. Another *extranjero* wishing to kick the ball. To my cautious eye they looked so formidable. *Hacktivistas y la presunción de inocencia.* White mink, silver fox, seagull soaring above the bay. More guys in ties prattling sacrifice. "Somos estudiantes, no maleantes," they chanted in the streets of Madrid. The Italian woman selling her possessions along the beach. Blue-gray sea swishing against the shore.

Self-definition depends on your definition of self, except when the state's involved. Though it couldn't be counted, it counted to us. Russia, o Russia, you know what I mean. A gate, a trailer, the wheelbarrow between us. All-purpose experts derailing the nation. I read "we" and my torso tightened. The journalist said he felt like a theater critic. Another white boy high on the merits of meritocracy. All these enzymes, the doctor whispered to herself. Where we worked in a currency of iron laws. Voting for the guy who fears God the most. The People's Republic of Zirconium redux. Little wooden birds were what we had left. Where energy-saving did not mean saving energy. The name of the firm was Mt. Hood Inc. Confidence men, confidence men, let down your golden hair. For his final meal on death row he requested diet cream soda. "America has a destiny in space. That's who we are," he said. Another cure for a yet unknown disease. I'm young enough for this shirt to be kitschy, right? *An urgent desire for a new beginning.* Putin a view to the future imperfect. Reflection a view to the silence in me.

✦SOURCES✦

Epigraphs
- Anahita Jamali Rad, *For Love and Autonomy* (Vancouver: Talonbooks, 2016), 79.
- Andrew Zawacki, *Video Tape* (Denver: Counterpath Press, 2013), 16.
- Claudia Rankine, *Citizen: An American Lyric* (Minneapolis: Graywolf Press, 2014), 155.
- Stuart Hall, "Culture and Power: Interview Stuart Hall," *Radical Philosophy*, 86, November/December 1997, 30.

Overdetermination Meets Polysemy in a Two-Fall-Ten-Minute-Time-Limit, Pay-Per-View Cage Match at the Convention Center in Portland, Oregon
- Michel de Certeau, *The Practice of Everyday Life*, Trans. Steven Rendell (Berkeley: University of California Press, 1984).
- "John Ruskin, An Introduction," Brantwood, Cumbria, UK, DVD, 1996.
- Henri Lefebvre, *The Production of Space*, Trans. Donald Nicholson-Smith (Oxford: Blackwell, 1991).
- Kaia Sand, Lecture on the poetics of walking, Oxford, England, 6 June 2009.

Silent Sting
- Robin Hahnel, *Green Economics: Confronting the Ecological Crisis* (Armonk, NY: M.E. Sharpe, 2011).
- Arundhati Roy, *Field Notes on Democracy: Listening to Grasshoppers* (Chicago: Haymarket Books, 2009).

"We Care About the Small People"
- "BP Chief: "We Care About the Small People," *Associated Press*, 16 June 2010, http://www.youtube.com/watch?v=th3LtLxOIEM
- Tim Webb, "BP Boss Admits Job on the Line Over Gulf Oil Spill," *The Guardian*, 13 May 2010.

Ode to Working Group II
- Vito Acconci, "Plot," 1974.
- Kathleen Hennessey, "Mitch Daniels Blasts Obama for 'Trickle-down Government'," *Los Angeles Times*, 24 January 2012.
- Intergovernmental Panel on Climate Change, "Summary for Policymakers," in *Climate Change 2007: Impacts, Adaptation and Vulnerability. Contribution of Working Group II to the Fourth Assessment Report of the Intergovernmental Panel on Climate Change*, M.L. Parry, O.F. Canziani, J.P. Palutikof, P.J. van der Linden and C.E. Hanson, Eds., Cambridge University Press, Cambridge, UK, 2007, pp. 7-22.
- On the Media, "Is Huffpost Good for Journalism?" *National Public Radio*, 29 April 2011.
- William Todd Schultz, *Tiny Terror: Why Truman Capote (Almost) Wrote Answered Prayers* (Oxford: Oxford University Press, 2011).

Fireworks
- Nicolas Bourriaud, *The Radicant* (New York: Lukas & Sternberg, 2009).
- Pablo Neruda, *Veinte Poemas de Amor y una Canción Desesperada* (Madrid: Alianza Cien, 1994).
- Bob Marley and the Wailers, "Bend Down Low."
- Dennis Brown, "No Speech No Language."
- Ujala Sehgal, "The Serious Implications of Stephen Colbert's FEC Stunt," *The Atlantic*, 14 May 2011.

Calling Tonya Harding
- "O Canada" (Canadian National Anthem.)
- Bob Marley and the Wailers, "Walk the Proud Land."

You Can't Stop Tiny Elvis
- Roy Miki, *There* (Vancouver: New Star Books, 2006).
- Rachel Zolf, *Neighbour Procedure* (Toronto: Coach House Books, 2010).
- Milton Friedman, *Capitalism and Freedom* (Chicago: University of Chicago Press, 2002 [1962]).

Upbeat Shakedown
- William Shakespeare, *Romeo and Juliet*.
- Boris Johnson, "Put a Sock in It, We're on to a Winner," *The Sun*, 20 July 2012.
- "BP or not BP? The Debut Performance of the Reclaim Shakespeare Company," http://www.youtube.com/watch?v=oMAlmPJHqHk&fe ature=player_embedded
- Mark Doidge, Conference on Sport, Leisure, and Social Justice, University of Brighton, 20 September 2013.
- Owen Gibson, "London 2012 Test Event Draws Polite Protest," *Guardian*, 4 July 2011.
- Image courtesy of Sally Brady.

Para Inglês Ver
- Collage materials from *Howler Magazine* and *Revista da História da Biblioteca Nacional*.
- Jules Boykoff, *Power Games: A Political History of the Olympics* (New York: Verso, 2016).
- Allison Cobb, *After We All Died* (Boise: Ahsahta Press, 2016).

Repository
- Nicholas Bourriaud, *The Radicant* (New York: Lukas & Sternberg, 2009).
- Susan M. Schultz, *Memory Cards: 2010-2011 Series* (San Diego: Singing Horse Press, 2011).

TINFISH

ALSO AVAILABLE FROM
TINFISH PRESS:

Ya-Wen Ho, *last edited [insert time here]*, 2012

Maged Zaher, *The Revolution Happened and You Didn't Call Me*, 2012

Jai Arun Ravine, แล้ว *and then entwine*, 2011

Elizabeth Soto, *Eulogies*, 2010

Kaia Sand, *Remember to Wave*, 2010

Daniel Tiffany, *The Dandelion Clock*, 2010

Paul Naylor, *Jammed Transmission*, 2009

Lee A. Tonouchi, *Living Pidgin: Contemplations on Pidgin Culture*,
2nd edition, 2009

Lisa Linn Kanae, *Sista Tongue*, 2nd edition, 2008

Craig Santos Perez, *from unincorporated territory [hacha]*, 2008 [out of print]

Meg Withers, *A Communion of Saints*, 2008

Hazel Smith, *The Erotics of Geography*, 2007

Linh Dinh, *All Around What Empties Out*, 2003, [out of print].
Subpress/Tinfish

Caroline Sinavaiana-Gabbard, *Alchemies of
Distance*. 2001, [out of print]. Subpress/
Tinfish/Institute of Pacific Studies

For other TinFish Press publications, including chapbooks and *TinFish* journals
1-20, visit our website: tinfishpress.com or order from spdbooks.org.

"I have this joke I've been trying to tell you." This refrain runs through *Fireworks.* The whole book is the "trying to tell." And the joke? It's us, the tragic absurdity of a species unable to stop self-destructing. The punchline lands with such tenderness, in language often achingly beautiful: "cardinals quivering on the concertina wire." These are poems only Jules could write—acts of witness at once outraged and playful. By his sheer creative wit he recalls for us the possibility of "that little place inside— unpoliceably mine."

—Allison Cobb

In *Fireworks*, Jules Boykoff has done what too many contemporary poets don't have the guts to do - stop writing! For a *long* while (poetic value capital stocks be damned!) until an authentic sense of agency lines up with the times. We don't know why or how exactly how it went down, but Boykoff did indeed pick up the pen again (while in Barcelona, Brighton, London, Vancouver, Rio de Janeiro) and strove to weave bits of his lived home life to globalism's storms as they rained down on the American Northwest. In this collection, one finds no catastrophism, no "revolutionary" pomp talk, and most certainly, no prideful quietism unto the social. The book is *sensitively* strident; each plod forward into the outer world feels like untrodden path- making. I'll go so far to say that I read *Fireworks* as an entirely new form of *under*-political victory waiting in the wings.

—Rodrigo Toscano

"The ruffle of a scrub jay's wings on landing" composed, the poem finds cadence flows and forms ever attentive to detail. Lending to the unruly and directly lived "we" across distance this work carries a robust kind of value. What is "unpoliceably" Jules Boykoff's *Fireworks* is relevant and integral. Here a sort of groundswell tends to soil to raise fact and fist. The work moves, as the poet has moved, through charges of smoke and spectacle. "Beauty and meaning bricked in misprision," the deterritorialized dream and nourish roots subject to amputation. Even when lost the phantom limbs lift and pick poetry blooms amid the festooned billows of perishable markets.

—Cecily Nicholson